Passion-Soaked Nerves

190 Songs of silent soul

NILANJAN DAS

-----1-----
What you did right
What you did wrong
Morning still bright
Forest black song
Chiseled cut curves
Wood craft smile
Passion-soaked nerves
Dream for a while!

-----2-----

I think to create more,
Away from all thoughts mind can make
While this dusk imagines dawn.

-----3-----
Desire guides again
Love curves stones of pain
King of hearts
Un-played parts
Known route unknown train.
Cold skinned morn fades in
Dream of a Goddess mise-en- scene
New found muse
Doodles let loose
Brown magic spell turns green!
You never needed no wealth
Unused thoughts preserved health
Little you knew
Bigger became you
Time playing game of stealth!

----------------4---------------------
There is no grace in speed
Slow dew drops I need
Meditative pause
Unexplained cause
Magic of time indeed!
Divine body of mind
Legs of root unkind
Sun kissed face
Abundant trace
Forgotten melody rewind!

------------5-------------------
I could see your soul
Sword sharp eyes play role
Kept on thinking
Dry lips sinking
Lost night neckline mole.
Meaning of your name
Broken rules of game
Sound of dawn
Pains long gone
True grace knows no shame!

-----6-----
Eyes still wait
Before reds turned green
A new tune for a scene
That smell before you left.
Nights wasted in sleep
Days digging deep
Crying morning returns
Unknown dream burns
I will not think but see
How a seed grows to be a tree!

---------------7--------------------
Faceless mindless dummies all around,
Lost in Justice verdict found.
This new morn's loud silence,
Paints red on blue with sharp grace!
Did you not know any time soon,
Truth will be revealed dark side moon?
Mass mind control looks easy game,
Will taste own pill back fired fame!
Who wins whose lose who deceives all?
When you rise up puppetry doll.
No point showing who can't see,
Mindless enjoy false victory!

---------------8--------------------
Thoughts glowing in dark
Dawn making its mark
Abundance smiles
Weekend morn shines
Swimming with highway shark!
Lips smiling deep
Bare ankles weep
Taking a pause
Forgotten cause
Love knows when to sweep!

-----------------9-------------------------
Game of alphabets
Naming unknown fates
Morning blues
False and trues
Opening closed gates!
Time teases time
Memories wind chime
Take the bus
Let it pass
Expectation crime!
Board game geek
Success plays trick
Ask no more
Let it pour
Week after week!

-----------------10-------------------
Beautiful Confusion
Mind boggling illusion
Lost purpose bed sheet
Softly lit coffee treat
Framing a needless thought
Seeing silence being fought
Time's call from known voice
Thinking again choosing choice!

--------------11--------------------------
A song for your eyes
Wrong question whys
Ripple paused lashes
Tear drop ashes
Long forgotten trip
Early morning grip
Hilly dark eve
Temple Road sleeve
Silence cries loud
Distance fools proud!

------------------12------------------------
 Faces are now names
Ten-digit games
Status update
Self-proclaimed fate
Notions never die
No one knows why
Questions never sleep
Answers hide deep
Rays on closed eyes
Winner morn sighs!

----------------13---------------------
Sunday morning Tea
Unsung folk melody
Black lines and red dream
Memories soft as cream
Shy soul rubbed known feet
Eyes closed all loud tweet
Take turn mock all fools
Madness smells like drools!

--------------14-----------------
Dropped Rose
Cropped pose
Mind map
Wine snap
Petal dream
Moonlit cream
Green on blue
Hidden clue!
Moment's grip
Memory trip!

----------------15-------------
Lights from a distant shore
Lot to say less or more
Looking back colors glow
Forgotten films motion flow!
Talking thoughts

Blocking thoughts
Alone soul
Faded goal!
Learn and do
Fro and to.

------------16--------
Frozen window of mind
Truth less time unkind
False dreams built on hope
Miseries end of rope
Fear I make you free
Laughter new born tree!
Time up afraid fraud
Come back long gone God!

-------------17------------------
Moments soaked in morning dream
Moist eyed road silent scream
Children die breathing shame
Grown ups still play old blame game!
Black hole moons in concrete sky
Gods are quiet who knows why?
Pouring more let all drown
Rainbows melting turning brown
Let me fall and flow with you
Away from game called false and true!

-----------18--------------------
This soft day seven years
Silence wrote frozen tears
Unknown joy touch of pain
Cloudy thoughts let it rain!
White is good doesn't fade
Minds play trick tailor made
Unknown trip to a once known land
Black coffee eve still waves hand!

-----------------------19---------------
Everything revolves while I sit still
When moments fall, I can feel,
Waiting and dreaming and falling in love
Giving much more than what I have,
Look around and collect your gift
Time wraps and hides if you can lift,
Still all rush who knows for what?
I still sit and play my part!

----------------20-----------------
Growing on leaps and bounds
Lots of thoughtless sounds
Wings of love you spread
Chains fall off like thread
Highway blues take rounds!
Packaging forms sans text
Secret code context
All reflections
Build perfections
Time guides what lies next!

--------------21-----------------
When you envisage
Open mind birdcage
Taking one step at a time
Little you knew
What once grew
Will morph silent wind chime!
Vulnerable little kitten thought
Mischievous believe it or not
Handle with care,
Don't let it dare
Tamper with focus you have got!

-------------22-------------------------
Learn to see, see to learn
Let it drip while you burn,
So many tales all around
If you read the silence of sound,
Close your eyes against the light
Lost memories shines bright!
Moments saved inside you
All you craved all that true
Paint in heart the place you saw
Long lost dreams can you draw?

--------------23--------------------
That look, too good to be true
Scrap book mind can you go through
Set all free fears you don't need
Burn them all unwanted weed !

let it fall
Let it glow
Growing tall
Moving slow
Puzzle cracked
Broken door
Truth unmasked
So much more!

-------------24--------------
Raindrop leaf
Unknown brief
Highway dream
Paused Sunbeam
Vibrant brown
Feather on crown
Surprised smile
Kills for a while
Lucky me fool
Handmade tool
Soft wet feet
Visual treat!

--------------25-----------------
Greedy grids
All she needs
Deadly grace
What a place
Baseline noon
Adolescent moon
Frozen eyes
Hows and whys
Backstreet souls
Sky high goals!
©Nilanjan Das

-------------26---------------
Looked at you with awe
Loved all created I saw
Butterfly chased morning light wind
Pigeon paused water feel pinned
Sun burned red smiled moon
Dark green feet glow noon
Opportunist mind seeks gold
Clay dry snow hides fold
Take a bow if you break rule
Preconceived mouths stay fool.

-----------27------------------

Today all we need
Sun soaked dream indeed
Unsaved poems die
Yellow petals lie
Climb and cross the wall
Disturbed mind's skull
Once time had tripped
Afternoon dripped
A friendly voiced called
All Nightmares stalled.
Fear wants to win
Later smiled Queen

Busy stalking leaf
Losing greater grief.

---------28-------------

Red dream morning cry
Passion found once dry
Clod skin salt summer bite
Memory smells smoke white
Heart shone top eyes cloud
Read mind distant loud
Feel touch take back gloom
Come close yet to bloom
That day still so fresh
Love left mind in creche
It's you you and you
Still I feel so new.

---------29--------------

Equinox noon frame by frame
Butterfly wind touches back and smiles
softly
unexpected call makes night younger.

----------30----------

Calcolaria afternoon yellow dust drops
Hungry red ache comes back once more
I will return before dusk.

-----------31-----------

Sovereign heart
Let me see
Sun green chart
All around me
Wish grown field
Dream draped path
Pampered shield
Warm moon bath.
Face I hide
Face I show
Fearless pride
Elements know.
Welcome back
Once lost faith
Found sound track
Joyous breath.

------------32----------

Equinox noon frame by frame
Butterfly wind touches back and smiles
softly,
Unexpected call makes night younger.

-----------33------------

Where I want to go,
There is no hurry till it arrives
The right train for me.

--------34------------

Path that knows no plot
Silent cloud gaze blot
Love her lust cream tone
Green dream lost sun lone
Price less stone warm smile
Spare me love for a while
This day I was born
Music found once torn
Write that tale and slay
Sparrow noon song let's play.

.

---------35-------------

I sat next to God
He stitched even though I wanted glue
Thread is durable he said

------------36------------

We laughed we laughed loud
Past information became knowledge of the
future
Green moment fell and dried.

-----------37--------------

Death dies still lives Passion
Dry veins resurrection
My path goes through you
Clod past bite so true.

Unknown You need me
Dreams you dare to see
Innocence knows no pause
Questions good enough cause.

Wet skin craves your teeth
Lost sleep underneath
Lust moaned afternoon
Well sung deep red moon.

-----------38------------

Light I learn from you
Truth shadow dance you do
Warm tone paints to heal
Found back once lost zeal
This day light years back
Light you've knew all lack
Days and nights you had made
Fools laughter made dark trade
You still teach to learn
Shadow minds light you earn
Visually deaf still lies
Light trance smiles and sighs.

-----------40--------------

Milkweed summer star bloom
Calotropis spoils all gloom
Purple wealth defines soul mate
When closed build your own gate.

Some life sleeps like a day
Night glows patterns you slay
Colors can sing and think
Seasons change before you blink.

Nature smart all around you
Knitting dreams nightmares too
If you know how to go close
She will pour passion on your toes.

---------------41----------------------

Early summer's warm breeze song
Kid Leaf griming found bloom long
I came back to pause for a while
Before leaving on a faded smile
Deep soft green be with me
Wanna smell moon while you see
Beats and tones stop me to write
Toddler words toothless bite
Stories I wish roots had saved
Come back summer eve once all craved.

------------42-------------------

Soft dead morning red
Spice dry moment's thread
Thoughts of love felt dawn
Breezy touched winter gone.

I knew we would meet
Dewsoft stone cold feet
Stood and waited long
Memories write love song.

Finger touch thought mind
Lost pain intertwined
Lips spoke something more
Eyes broke once shut door.

-------------43-----------------

Mind still grows like tree
Loves dream touch cloud free
Canvas paradise blue
Mind still has no clue.

Age old trick mind plays
Known gaze silence slays
Lonely branches fall
Mind fools unwind calls.
Sky don't feel no pain
Unbound lost story chain
Déjàvu dusk light face
Roots I need your grace.

------------44--------------------

Shadow of light on wood
Shadow they speak no good
Lights change space shadow moves
You stay same, time grooves.

Forms and shapes shadow dance
Each odd day brings chance
Who cares what all think
Shadow loves when lights blink.

Stories you love shadow tells
Childhood dreams ring bells
Shadow can take all blows
Till you rise light glows.

-----------45-------------

Summer evening's goal
Orange moon black hole
Purple light
Lost tale night
Time plays puppeteer's role.

Who knows who will win
Lost sun stays within
Madness shouts
Cleaning doubts
Let's write song deep green.

Not a good finisher type
Descending goes on a hype
Odd ascending gloom
Neon dark roads still bloom
Old song knows no swipe

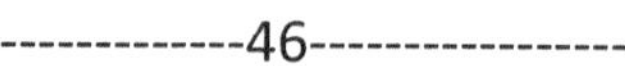
-------------46-----------------

Body listened while I slept
Till REVOLUTION started again with eyes
closed
Yin and yang still plays.

-----------47---------------

Looked at you with awe
Loved all created I saw
Butterfly chased morning light wind
Pigeon paused water feel pinned

Sun burned red smiled moon
Dark green feet glow noon
Opportunist mind seeks gold
Clay dry snow hides fold
Take a bow if you break rule
Preconceived mouths stay fool.

.

----------48-------------------

Today all we need
Sun soaked dream indeed
Unsaved poems die
Yellow petals lie
Climb and cross the wall
Disturbed mind's skull
Once time had tripped
Afternoon dripped
A friendly voiced called
All Nightmares stalled.
Fear wants to win
Later smiled Queen
Busy stalking leaf
Losing greater grief.

.

------------49--------------

Silence more than my attention
Memories were made for prevention
Lost and found
Homeward bound
Worthless kinds of attraction.
Standing next to my shadow,
In timeless waiting in a deep meadow
Unfolding Joy of a place
In sudden found grace
Breathing moments of life still fallow

Path knows your destination
Trust and move without hesitation
Less you know
More you Flow
Dream like a moment's satisfaction.

--------------50--------------------

Fallen but still not dead
She will bring change in your thoughts
Stone can't spoil her grace.

---------------51-------------------

Eyes closed
Bow body still stay awake
Senses aroused
Chakras connect like snake. .
Deep dark eyes
Agile ancient Queen
Silence cries
Beauty like never seen.
Once far
Now I feel you near
Together
Let's make joy force shear.

------------52------------

Just few strokes of led
Parable kept unread
Soul you meet and feel
Time moves back time wheel.

Win and lose game ends
Unfollow no need trends
Found and lost once more

Sketchbook dreams night shore.

Wicked Darkness stalks
Time guards stray eve rocks
Pencil still loves shape
Eyelash night blue Cape.

-----------53--------------

Blind mind can see now
Brown may turn green how
Hateful morphs desire
Sun breeze thought song fire.
Body of mind knows truth
Fly back widows' youth
Cramp soul needs green fluid
Silence brings cool druid. .
Take a break for break though
Plan may have plans too,
Dark makes love to light
Time blooms new insight.

-----------54-----------

Dry leaf drowns
Holiday browns
Moment's pause
Cherished cause.
Nothing stays
Parting ways
Clouds on path
Wet sunbath.
Morning sleep
Dream soak deep
Soul mate's smile
Time makes tile.
Thoughts you choose
Mind let loose.
Stop and see, sleeping tree.

-----------55---------

When you read me
I do read you too
Page leaf unknown tree
Word face say all true.
Chapters all kept safe

Still you fail to read
Bookmarks hide dark Cape
Thoughts dry monologue seed.
Walk and pause and write
Then read what you see
Together we shall bite
Reader and Book beastie.

-------56---------

Call from a soul silent,
Name sake game time spent
Warmth of blue, ground away glue
Close to dream that meant.
Further far you go
Eyes shut you may show
Black you wear, white you swear
Heart feels truth you know.
Fear of past flashback
Wasn't that bad enough sack?
Warm dusk air, golden glare
Thoughtless mind you lack.

------57---------

Down the memory lane song
Nothing was same neither me nor you
Mind still loves to remember.

-------58------------

For how long can you?
Every time you resist, I rediscover strength
Vulnerability can be so sensuous.

-------59--------

Mid night's woke up dream
Have never lost you thoughts brought joy
Thanks but I need more.

-------60---------

Now I see you dawn
Lost dark night was just an illusion
Destination whispered joy and bloomed.

------61---------

Through me you keep creating
Hollow green ego grows stronger each
moment
Light will burn all someday.

--------62---------

I will pick my lights
From all crack holes in every darkness
Dreamers don't doubt in self.

-------------63-------------------------

We made stars in the sky
Never thought any reason why
We made stars in the day
Time had so much more to say.

Now we make sale buy and sale
Reasons got blunt weak and pale
Cherished love still draws stars bright
Moment's fun preserved borrowed sight.

We could still find no reason laugh

Take a flight each other's behalf
Not counting every little gain
Let's draw stars all over again.

Lines of dream dipped paint
Trip to tear-soaked song so known
Wet brush kissed your feet

=================================

-----64------

And then you came
Like a thoughtless name
All I knew meant much more
Message in a bottle left lost shore.

Better we go with this flow
Orange soft summer's sudden found glow
Taking time before frozen time lapse
Magic hour mind broken door flaps.

Broken dream again fights cruel doubt
Notion false never needed put on pout
Reading heartfelt no recent past
Now is yours all that will last.

---------------65------

Plastic light we take
Busking together fake
Captive dreams can fly
Love can still ask why.

.

Love loves give all game
No need absurd shame
Break free dive away deep
Life will hold green grip.

Teach self-thinking bright
Attract all starry night
When you wake with smile
Nectar lips my aisle.

--------70----------

Sunday canvas stroke
Touch once lost and broke
Past you don't need now
Answers found anyhow.

Dreams you gave away then

Kept on counting ten
Journey you thought known
Stranger called on phone.

Not a group you need a team
Seven hues one sunbeam
Magic you make and live
One more Sunday weave.

-------71---------

I need not judge but heal
Free from past cloud deal
Eyes closed open my vision
One drop Sun submission. .
Now all true friends come
Love for no reason sum
Mythical mind goodbye
Don't need answer why.
.

Give me a patch of green
Bedtime silver screen
Touch my soul so deep
Purple crown may weep.

----72------

Nothing dries dead
It's all in your head
Resist no song
Soul soft strong. .
Beige lone eyes
Teardrop dries.
Nose ring moon
Passion lips June.
.
Before dream drops
Glowing eve crops
Play it once more
Lost tune score.

-----73--------

Analema Sun dream loop
Time gives one more scoop
Song you hate to love
Comes back once lost Dove.
Can't I make her stay
Life will find a way
Mistakes once you've felt

Self grudge shall all melt.
Float with grace don't rush
Paint love without brush
Hint will come and show
When where how to go.

-----74--------

Frames of mind within
Out of Mise-En-Scene
Known light skin unknown
Post thought frame outgrown.

Need unneeded clean
Dream will let you glean
Time shows right time hint
New way life imprint.

We get what we want
Focus on breath of chant
Take black when white gone
Checkmate surprise pawn.

------75--------

Time shows manyatimes
Decoded love windchimes
Reflection your grey
Prettiest glass morn prey.
Now I see through light
Whispered past song flight
Trailers time showed then
Your shine bleached all stain.
Songs I wrote and lost
Your brown gaze deep frost
Got back all in a flow
Zen eyed flute shine glow.

-----------76------

Your red had to wait
Till I found time's bait
Nothing gone summer bloom
Monsoon dream drenched all gloom.
Restless mind stupid child
Poking thoughts running wild.
Every drop stored for me
Hidden song Old friend tree.
Vision blurred patch of green

Waited long silver screen.
Shutting mouth loving wind
Tell me more my Reem hind.

-------77---------

Dark mind wet and cold
Time guards path unfold
Past shines paradise fool
Answers drip glass tool.
Who said don't think that
What's being said right at
Are you listening right
Darkness makes lights bright.
You knew still wrong route
Wrong right forbidden fruit
Eve melts drop by drop
All yours new born crop.

------78-------

Are you still in one piece
A day is all you cease
Tracks stay back train moves
Red Toy face time grooves.

See what's being shown
Stay little longer zone
Unknown mind speaks rude
Observe lone crow dude.
Do what can't be done
Let grilled eve head spun
Old city dream will bloom
Another night loves gloom.

-------79-------

Problems you gave dark
Same old way they lark
Now I solve them right
God of Red shines bright.
Hard work answers all
Tedious mind stops fall
God smiles deep inside
Go on enjoy ride.
Entered needed path
Drops of Red moon bath
Mind don't spoil my view
World in a drop of dew.

--------80-------

Concrete wing
Drenched cold zing
Paused for a while
One more mile
Move on glass
Smooth flow class.
Lucky you gut
Low sword cut
Enjoy stroke
Dream un broke
Disguised boon
Late learned soon.
So many minds
No needed finds
Music stays
Blues on greys
Rain brings on
All pain gone.

------81------

Take a pause Monster Mind
You non believer kind
Luck smiled and said Hi
Stop all doubtful cry.
Queen of my dream town
Does not like your frown
Mystery spot intuition
Let's start new discussion.
Soul finds another soul
Success without goal
Deep dark eyes spread wing
Song I love to sing.

-------82------

Midnight's call
Dream leaves fall
Makes you feel the need
Miles you go
Sink in flow
Story to be told indeed.

Lost love found

Raindrop sound
Time will take you there
Go for it
Power Day treat
Use your self-built flair.
Body knows all
Let fear fall
All is good and strong
Problems turn
Let it burn
Rights born from all wrong.

-------83--------

Like a moth to a flame
Drawing you making tame
You felt good looking down
Now my turn proud dead town.
.

When you thought what a catch
Chocked my soul pulling latch,
Battle you want you'll get,
Last laugh all I need mate.

.

Someone had to stop you snob,

Let me turn you into a blob,
No longer you can suffocate,
Music of life will resonate.

-----84-------

Let me feel this blue
Head less lost mind clue
Body floats Fearless grind
Below the surface kind.

Doing whatever body wants
Feeling good factor stunts
Not being a doormat though
Shell door unlocked blow.

Swimming in intuition
Remaining calm in fusion
Silence makes loud noise
Let time speak my voice.

------85-------

No shortcut for the best
Charismatic leap reaches crest,
Play at the top
Daydream drop
Time for action fest.
.

Tricky will be this game
Unfair feels no shame,
Quit if you feel
It's your zeal
That will make you a name.
.

Such an arrogance - they say
No attention you pay
You will know
Which way to go
When dawn reveals the day.

-------86-------

Good will bloom
When I change
Self made gloom
Mind rearrange. .
Music heals
Let it grow
Worry thought steals
Distant throw.

Highway Sun
Loves grey cloud
All or none
Sing out loud.

Pink on green
Baby leaf eyes
Silver screen
Knows all Whys.

----87-----

Myself I and me
Together stay we three,
Stay close when in need
Enjoy lucky day breed.

.

Distant unknown call
Makes you instant fall
When all three can't make
All alone chance don't take.

.

Distant past may haunt
Ignore tasteless taunt
When time shapes us three
Read all clues for free.

------88---------

Bulbul breeze paints dark clouds
Forgotten music knocks on six strings soul
Time to fly once more.

-------89-------

Let the new born guide
Evaporated past changes now drop by drop
Help me to unlearn all.

--------90------

Oleander bud take my word
Loud angry green needs your red joy
Learn from fearless bloom child.

Feeling need to slow down
Stealing greed of lost town
Love I give
Passionate weave,
Shut your eyes to soak brown.
You talk sad and sugar falls
Feel good minds answer calls.
Now I see
Your blue tee
Shines with smile heart trolls.
Tears can bring much joy
Kid Bro morn loved toy.
Your tone
Pleasured moan
Want you more Goddess Floy.

--------92---------

Let the Light enter
Mind stay in center
Guitar strings
Joy she brings
Assumption creates epicenter.

Why shall I bother and think?
Un-promised hold that blink
Red lips gaze
Shy love craze
Moment's voice sends lost link.

Ready to fly once more
See you soon happy shore
Smog and cloud,
All think loud
Once closed unlocked door.

-------93----------

Dry leaf drowns
Holiday browns
Moment's pause
Cherished cause.

Nothing stays
Parting ways
Clouds on path
Wet sunbath.

Morning sleep
Dream soak deep
Soul mate's smile
Time makes tile.

Thoughts you choose
Mind let loose.
Stop and see
Sleeping tree.

-------94------

Blind mind can see now
Brown may turn green how
Hateful morphs desire
Sun breeze thought song fire.
Body of mind knows truth
Fly back widows youth
Cramp soul needs green fluid
Silence brings cool druid.
Take a break for break though
Plan may have plans too,
Dark makes love to light
Time blooms new insight.

-------95--------

Light at the tunnel's end
Say no to darkness loud and clear
Time to do the known.

------96--------

Just few strokes of led
Parable kept unread
Soul you meet and feel
Time moves back time wheel.
.

Win and lose game ends
Un follow no need trends
Found and lost once more
Sketchbook dreams night shore.
.

Wicked Darkness stalks
Time guards stray eve rocks
Pencil still loves shape
Eyelash night blue Cape.

--------97--------

Eyes closed
Bow body still stay awake
Senses aroused
Chakras connect like snake. .

Deep dark eyes

Agile ancient Queen
Silence cries
Beauty like never seen.

.

Once far
Now I feel you near
Together
Let's make joy force shear.

-------98-------

Now I see your bloom
Even when you're still a bud
Visionary takes away gloom
Morn Moon shines on mud.
My lost soul knew none
Your quiet eyes spoke though
Time stopped useless spun
Showed all I should know.

Want none stop none mode
Full of bliss I feel,
Destined to be on road
Once more time loop wheel.

-------99--------

Can't look away from you,
Eyes froze and heart too
On your drape morning shines
Royal green forgotten wines

Gratitude mind full of love
Thank you smile soft dream dove
Silence sings Symphony pause
Desired lust not known cause.

Mahalaya chant divine thought
Memories love all dead knot
Back in town forth in time
Story of us lost wind chime.

-------100-----

Escaped for a long departure
Vibration speaking of exotic nature
Horizon new
Soaked in dew
Gratitude melts stiff ego caricature.
Observe self all day long,
Unplanned trip unheard song
Golden cloud
Green dream loud
Flame in heart still burns so strong.
Passionate love longs desired spice
Business frame of mind advice
Fulfilling time
Silent mime
Admired soul feels touched and wise.
Brown lips stain on shoulder white
Deep dark black gaze noon like bright
Nothing is lost
Love melts frost
Talkative poetry sleepless night.

-------101-------

Coffee shadow Sun glow morn,
Blends all lone and torn
Monk wall canvas wet
Fortune tells no threat.

Unknown just mind state,
No mind no ill fate
Let light enter full
Life boat needs no pull.

Decision makes your luck,
Give Gratitude when stuck
Unknown Sunlight smile
Feel good life for a while.

------102------

Lost in inner world
Gratitude green pearled
Music calls in dream
Let the Seeker find
Unseen unwind
Success needs no scream.

Feel before you get
Love fruit target
Knowing all coming your way.
Eye for detailing
Wide shut remaining
Body moves while mind stay.

Bloom seed I saw
Tomorrow's line draw
Answers hide inside.
Just feel grateful
That's a magic tool
Makes my wish joy ride.

-------103-------

Come sit in my blue heart
Some wit clue the fly art
You came and stood by
Quite a game of known why.
.

I need no words sound

Mind speaks body spellbound
Found in you all I needed soul
Silence smiles attraction goal.

Come and find me one more time
Some place else in a new rhythm
Your groove on my song
Rights will love making wrong.

--------104---------

Sunbeam on your back
Mind path lost all track
Throat dry glow shut eyes
Truth sang goodbye lies.

I ran out for air
Even crossed forbidden stair
You asked how did I know
Loved your ankleted toe.

Enchanted night eyes

Silent moon still cries
How I felt you know
Warm love still melts snow.

-------105------

New look face grown old
Together found lost gold
Memories winter noon
Still draws Christmas toon.

Weekend's comic con
Tales of darkest dawn
Wearing geeky black band
Why time can't still stand?

Young one wants more time
Grandma wrote young rhyme
Childhood sweetheart tale
Emotions not for sale.

--------106-------

Psychic chakra strong
Easy flow smoothes all wrong,
Desires grow
Sun's soft throw
Warm hue forgotten song!

Grey hair time grows fine,
Priceless charm old wine,
Don't you rush
Soft kiss hush
Morning's dream touch shine!

Tell me why you cried?
Heart loved voice still lied!
Lost not a thing,
Still I sing,
Songs we kept aside.

-------107------

Introspection time,
Forgotten once known rhythm ,
Wakeup now
Life's strong bough
Has been your guide prime!

New bud knows his flow
Dark sky makes star glow,
Let him fall
Follow your call
Joyful beat grows slow.

Universe loves you right
Fearless take off flight
Signs are sent
For you meant
Calyx holds you tight.

-------108-----

Anger attacking Bear
Pedophile red nightmare,
Touch me oh soft light,
Melts ego, widens sight.

Insecure mouth lies
Masked friendship act dies,
Morning raga infant
Breeze note close distant. .

Hand is such a great tool,
Designed to break all rule,
Come and flow through palm
While I enjoy calm.

------109-------

Older month younger year,
Foggy morn mind still unclear,
Olive Sun finds new route,
One more bite forbidden fruit.

Love this path's wilder smell,

Tender noon fantasy spell,
Holding hands walking slow,
Sit for a while let time glow!

Brewing dream I can't kill,
Instant joy loves my bill,
Looking back from the end,
Desires typed just click send!

-------110------

Time needs time Some more,
Meanwhile reach deep core,
Looked away all life far,
Now found you my near! .
Democracy seems old joke,
Millennium still burns smoke,
Love those secular lies,
Karma wipes all cries! .
Fools abuse and chant,
Hollow pride's all-day rant,
This blue Sunbeam touch,
Time wants me to clutch.

-------111-------

Memories yesterday,
Tomorrow's thought made way,
Hostel room paradise,
Music makes you wise.
Joy and wishful light,
Fearful thoughts kept quiet,
Silent smile unknown,
Soft depth of field zone.
Answers laid so close,
Arrogant questions rose,
Hash tag awaited long,
Now smile once loved song!

---------112-------

Power, I feel,
Raw strength deal,
My art shines,
Soul gold mines.
Payback time,
Grudge less prime,
Dignity calls,
Dream stop trolls.

Muse still guides,
Passionate wides,
Love your pause,
Be my cause!

-----113------

Blessed dreams take my praise,
My eyes see you raise,
Hunter mind knows pause,
My dream my life's cause!

Now I know your name,
Age old silent game,
Morning skin touch thought,
Songs of Joyful knot! .

Green shadow loves your look,
Sweet home dry leaf book,
My path leads to you,
My dream soft born dew!

-----114-----

Gone past dead goodbye,
Thought leaf unwant dry,
Last night's brown do change,
Look through vision's Orange.
Music feels no time,
EQ's unsolved crime,
Melodies take you back,
Love tale unlost track.
Evening's lustful weep,
Always stayed so deep,
I don't need no proof,
Known your unseen roof.

-------115-------

Shot my monkey mind,
Hunter dream unkind,
Numbness rest in peace,
Defeated all enemies.
Back story flashback pain,
Sinful all Hell's gain,
Choose thoughts make luck shine,
Animal doubt sleeps fine.

Long way long term plan,
Grow your strength my clan,
Darkness your soul mate,
Once you reach Star gate!

-----116------

Stand by what is right,
Your life that's your fight,
Know and speak your need,
Self care deed indeed.
Truth and knowledge you seek,
Fearful makes you weak,
Wish and go with flow,
Gratitude makes you glow.
Decoded folklore vibe,
Needless dogfight tribe,
Chakras make your link,
Spectrum love let's drink!

-------117---------

Nine realms kept you strong
Darkness lost all wrong
One each away from all
Nine books secret call.

You came look and found
Time chose one more round
Woke me from my death
Deep gaze took my breath.

Arrows and bow I made
Not a gift curse instead
Take my soul and burn
That's your clue my turn.

----118-----

Walk away with the stream,
Walk away morning dream,
Goodbye naysayers all,
Walk away follow your call.
Know what you don't need,
Mood board planted seed,
Hearing leaves and roots,
Body knows what best suits!
Reflection all see,
Music still grows tree,
Walk away from closed door,
Life means so much more!

----119----

Formless Lavender green,
Mind shell cracked path screen,
Karmic passionate clash,
Truth created in a flash.
Past present future lost,
Consciousness all cost,
Let mind branches find,
While body roots unwind. .
Spring fruits ripe and dry ,
Shape less dreams still try,
Supreme rests in less,
Look within always!

----120-----

I see sound in silence,
How life grows now make sense,
Inside outside all one,
Lights cause free will darkness. .
Distant past like bokeh dot,
Memories' dry brunch scar thought,
Useless math bugs night's day,
Screen play knew all screen shot.

One tree we are all part,
When you end then I start,
Shred leaves detaching desire,
Body knows one soul attire!

---------121--------

No longer feel squeezed,
Shift identity released,
Wakeup reality kind,
Life time span body mind.
Memories clarity gained,
Victim freed unchained,
Sensorial delight,
Perception takes flight.
Visionary mind now quiet,
Access brings insight,
Desires of becoming,

Now "Be" that one thing.

------122------

Forceful positive mind,
Worse than negative kind,
Not known limited bar,
Quiet heads go beyond star.
Stillness joy brings glow,
Effortless clarity's flow,
Be aware moment's presence,
Pick state importance. .
Self-history holds back,
Mind makes universe track,
Create a new world zone,
Put life back in stone!

------123------

As I go more close,
Awestruck morning shows,
More than what I knew,
Love shines Gratitude dew.
Proud petals gone dry,
Blame game shallow mind's cry,
Wish I knew more less,
All search ends in guess.
Magical silence bloom,
Glory shreds away all gloom ,
Grays will turn in green ,

Oneness all over screen .

-----124------

Power of formless form,
Live green rustic storm,
Needless put on dream,
Formless forms new stream.
No point explain tool,
Surprised successful,
Blurred past dark zone guild,
Softens depth of field. .
Roots move new shapes fill,
All moves nothing is still,
Deep within black hole,
Formless peace you stole .

-----125-------

More Eyes more or less ,
Truth is just wild guess,
Face paints once broke heart,
Confront before you start. .
Ageless mind infant,
New place likes instant,

Be in now look around,
Let past have a sleep sound. .
Innocent evening game,
Look alike tales not same,
It's your turn play on,
Write down before its gone.

-------126-----

World less known,
Daydream zone,
Takes me back always,
Thoughts Black ink,
Makes you sink,
Crack code what it says.
Secret house,
Untraced browse,
Seen in sleep closed eyes ,
Lost path need,
Found indeed,
Answers all your Whys. .
Standing by,
Hope soft dry,
Knows me inside out,
Hides within ,
Strength Unseen ,
Nine world's goal undoubt .

-------127-----

Self love soft eyes dark,
Green shines found lost spark,
Soul sleeps heart restless,
Hold back loud silence. .
Thoughts write luck all day,
Unknown mind makes way,
Teach me not to guess,
Look for loud silence. .
Body hides map of joy,
Treasure hunt age old toy,
Unsolved found no trace ,
Need my loud silence.

-----128-----

Brown soft young wet day,
Miracle droplet slay,
Now heart desires none,
Green stem still grows Sun.
Umbrella noon sleepy eyes,
Ant's trail on glass sighs,
Feet stalled heads rush though,
Brown kiss go with flow.
Blurry past taught silence,
Purple eve intense,

Brown green then again brown,
Dream drops feather on crown.

-----129-------

Dry brush morning stroke,
Toxic spell once broke,
Reflection still wet,
Purpose now you get.

When we had no clue,
Stayed along morning blue,
Frame by frame love songs,
Less rights loved more wrongs.

Now look back and say,
Rolls we hate still play ,
Let's meet lost time's sake ,
New vive lost mistake.

-----130----

Get out of gloomy mode,
Green fruit passionate code,
Big world kept in store,

Get out and explore. .
Happiness decision made,
Observe life instead,
Time grows out of time,
Storm breaks age old rhythm. .
Life will grow more lives,
Known fruit unknown vibes,
Let them troll and talk,
While your roots break rock.

------131------

One last look.
Before you're plucked,
Wet wind shook,
Nectar sucked.
Dream drops hang,
From my wing,
Known cell rang,
Morph and swing. .
Change and bloom,
Soul found love,
Light-year's gloom,
New song Dove.

-------132-----

Goodfellas good morning,
Any bell does it ring?
Your you looks at you,
While sky paints more blue.
Black turns grey turns white,
Unwind mind loves bright,
Feet rests heart moves on,
Child eyes stay awake dawn.
Grow organic joy,
Enough of dated ploy,
Look with love and see,
Goodfellas goodtime glee.

-----133-----

For your mind,
Play along ,
Flow song ,
Don't rewind. .
Soft dark noon,
Time blinks,
Lost links,
Disguised boon.
Get start mode,

Now say,
Break away,
Naysayer's code!

Parallel worlds met once,
Spoke of dreams, took chance,
Sat till known sundown,
Unsung notes left town.
Selfish success scream,
Dreamers lost not dream,
That will bring them back
Following forgotten track. .
Once known now stranger,
Close clouds drifted far,
Karma's complete task,
Same team new found mask.

-----135------

Best kept secrets shine,
Life still goes on fine,
Time keeps silent clues ,
Dawn burns morning blues. .
Laugh at anxious rush ,
Last rain's new found crush ,
Deep eyed soft dark gaze,
Dream more new born craze.
Take me back once more,
Beyond the long closed door,
Once I fly and land,
New song for a new band.

-----136------

One more story untold,
Glittering midnight gold,
Morning's bokeh star smile,
Take a pause breath for a while.
Can you brand a place?
Away from shallow rat race,
Race I lose to win,
Terracotta flame glows skin.
Guitar cried whole eve,

Tunes we need to weave,
It's all there for you,
Take a pause unfold clue.

------137------

Strokes and lines says more,
More than mind can store,
Go apart shadow night's dream,
Till this parable's stream! .
Carbon melts in thoughts,
Tie loose once felt knots ,
Let's talk one on one,
Mob mind clue less gun.
Alphabets remain,
Words now mean no pain,
Innocent love let burn ,
Warrior soul mate's turn.

------138------

Moon shadow blue cityscape,
Lone park story escape,
You search what you know,
Look within soft glow! .

I don't say but see,
Write and sing for me,
Song that loves dark night,
Eyes stay awake mind quiet. .

Mind once lost my Moon,
Will find any time soon,
Time that paints blue cloud,
Cloud that plays song loud.

-------139-------

Purple shadow of dawn,
Kachnar dream bud spawn,
Bless me passionate glow,
Love undressing slow! .
Orchid morning kiss,
Unknown song you miss,
Stay for a while and pause,
Paint more no effect cause. .
Young breeds shows me how,
Body guides block mind now,

Search won't stop my heart,
Time now adds to cart!

------140------

Explore comfort zone,
Destiny gratitude stone,
Backyard's unknown bloom,
Sun burns last night's gloom.
Sky taught take your time,
Silence makes sound mime,
This day won't come back,
Seize all heart can stack.

------141`--------

Sit here wait all day,
All time I have may,
Life paused and took turn,
I shine while you burn!

For a cause I was sent,
Learning what life meant,
Live now just for a day,
Let life show me way!

Morning's green dreams shine,
Memories wait old wine,

Goalless growth makes sense,
Blue wings wait intense!

--------142---------

Here I bloom again,
Forgetting yester's pain,
Once you have found me,
Answer drops softly.

Questions you don't need,
Fear mind useless weed,
Let joy shine instead,
Dreams reborn once dead.

No matter who says what,
Wheel of life moves smart,
White light broke all gloom,
Soft kissed loved my bloom!

---------143----------

Ravishing radiant pause,
Spread wings heartfelt cause,
My voice kissed your dream,
Unknown be my stream!

Take a walk one more time,
Thinking big no crime ,
Sun kissed softness glows,
Soule mate music flows! .

Give any name you feel,
Name less joy my deal,
Known from another birth,
Love knows time's true worth!

-----144-----

Spread winged Phoenix moment,
Dry red dreams arrogant,
Unique you are one,
Together let's burn Sun!
Red moon cried and left,
Soft dawn forgotten theft,
Repeated age old pain,
Make love redefined stain!
Thought writes lips smile quiet,
Heartfelt gaze all might,
Feel this one more day ,
Let this new love stay!

-----145-----

My dream sleeps and glows,
Love felt heart stills flows,
Need your nectar all,
Poppy night's silent call,
You have my lost part,
All my secret art,
Passionate eve knows all,
Poppy night's silent call.
Drag me towards light,
Kiss soaked blue moon's bright,
Memories moan grace fall,
Poppy night's silent call !

-----146-----

I flow and stay still,
Read life's mystic will,
Unbend long strong head,
Well known but all dead.
I know I don't rush,
New paint loves old brush,
Let the light guide dark,
I flow with life's arc !!
Soft cloud mind minds lot,
Mindless flow stops thought,

Now time helps unblock,
Dream awakes my paused clock!

-----147-----

Take a moment's pause,
Gaze at creation's cause,
For a reason here you are,
Miracle made this far.
You are what you seek,
Undermining meek,
Attract success verse,
Dream blooms from dried curse !
Power of No grows now,
No matter who tries how,
Boundless beauty stays,
Love finds souls always!

-----148-----

When you begin from small,
They say all that you are not,
You know what you know.

-------149------

Life feels so light and new,
Nightmares gone from where fear grew.
There grows new hope and more,
Show me what else kept in store.
Words flow and fly like song,
Magical mind makes me soft and strong
,
Yellows born from mature appetite
green,
I am all ears Decalogue script to screen.
Need to start once stopped parable
walk,
Peace mind smiles at unknown stalk,
I bloom in dark when heart shines like
morn,
Let's paint new tint on time's old page
torn.

---------150------

Asymmetric mind looks for chaos,
Unknown morning provokes to fall in
love,
Tilted frame hangs like past.

------151------

Dead rose afternoon,
Imperfection boon,
Longed for you all along,
Sweet pain unheard song.
More than love heart feels,
Unsaid wild night grills,
Where eyes can't see more,
Passionate memory's store .
Mediocrity all around,
Blabbering same old sound,
Dream dew changes fate,
Time breaks once locked gate.

--------152-----

I am sorry my monster,
Please forgive me,
For I was your creator,
Lost identity.
I summoned sorrows and worries of all,
Gratitude angel distant call,

Unhappy mind now cloudy and dark,
My shattered dream lost all it's spark
New month begins with old habits,
Memory smiles love pieces and bits,
New found joy is like passion Sun,
Goodbye my monster we are done.

-----153-----
Testimony to the light,
Follows the darkest night,
Metamorphosis name,
Goodbye age-old shame.

Love felt at first sight,
Your eyes morning's bright,
Found path that took few,
Showed me all I knew.

Conflicts all within,
Made my shape unseen,
Death makes rebirth call,
Grateful for it all.

-----154-----
Now I look within,
Fears won't stay unseen,
Reclaim and realign,
Clean my purpose shine.

As I go more close,
Awestruck morning shows,
More than what I knew,
Love shines gratitude dew.

Proud petals gone dry,
Blame game shallow mind's cry,
Wish I knew more less,
All search ends in guess.

Magical silence bloom,
Glory shreds away all gloom,
Greys will turn in green,
Oneness all over screen.

-----155------
Be in a state of no thought,
Whole body feels like one dot,
You see more than you know,
Take sip time juice let go.
When your hand just draws line,
Eyes see in awe soul shine,
Manipulators try very hard,
All headlines seem absurd.
When whole world is unknown,
Why care name game dark zone,
Imagine and dream all day,
While in right now you stay.
------156-----
White butterfly dawn,
Eternal music sworn,
Insight shown,
Once unknown.
Your body knew life's purpose,
While greener looked other side's grass,
Then came one white messenger,
Wake up now known stranger.
Reboot yourself, relocate,
Joyful thoughts will change fate,
Like minded heart's symphony,
Goodbye lone night's agony.

-----157-----
Be here be alone my green new leaf love,
Shadow of soul has gone for forgotten dove,
I will be back at dry brush winter's end,
Unbox passionate dark red soft kiss trend.
Chaotic city life online soul massacre,
Peace of mind now left with endless scar,
Dream kept torn stem dipped in nectar vase,
Come my muse now tell me who I was.
Many more light years we shall cross together,
Away from fake loud mouths of same old feather,
No goal just I want to be with you more,
Known Shadow solitude silent music shore.

-----158-----
You are where you need to be,
Failures bring more victory,
Spring Sunbeam will wake up soon,
Spread your wings for morning moon.
Mystic doors are opening slow,
Heartfelt love makes your lips glow,
Silent eyes tell thousand words,
More than time wrote on my cards.
Colors change that's the rule,
Forget all that old school,
Let's write and sing lines few more,
Passionate crave will start to pour.

-----159-----

Let go you from "You",
No matter what says who,
How can lost be found?
Truth was safe and sound.

Pause and feel the soul,
Many worlds but one goal.

Stick around let joy guide,
stand by your own side.

Look for clues unknown,
Mind speaks guidance shown,
Follow dreams unlock mode,
That's you and your code.

-----160-----

You thought roots will hold,
Inner world has grown beyond your
imagination,
You now grow new roots.

-----161-----

Dream within a dream,
Endless soft torn scream,
You came now you're gone,
Shadow cloud melts to morn.
Come light let's play a game,
New tale for old name,
No matter who says what,
Don't stop once you start.

They thought they know you,
Truth smiled soaked in dew,
Take time world moves slow,
Go deep let dream glow.

-----162-----
Lines of thoughts and dreams,
You float while ego screams,
My muse tell me more,
Mind's tale kept in store.
Ink blue sometimes black,
Light will pass through crack,
Till then we shall dance,
Life drops moment's chance.
Shots of you brings joy,
Lost lane forgotten toy,
Love sings morning breeze,
Fly high leave known trees.

-----163-----
Waking up inside a dream,
Memory from the past birth finds me,
Your flame in my eyes.
-----164-----
When all this war ends,
Shadows of life will find us again,
To tell a new tale.

-----165-----
Don't go deep they say,
Hollow lives float all day,
Answers sleep and hide,
While I laugh deep and wide.
I saw your mind map,
Headless body pride cap,
Shameful history's pride,
Still, I laugh deep wide.
You thought I will fight,
On wrongs you've made right,
But time showed flip side,
Taught me to see deep wide.

-----166-----
This had to happen.
Many more nights, and gloomy days
ago.
My seed waited and dreamt.
Now your bud is ready, and so am I.
Your nectar will soon spread, through
my lips.
We will take it slow.
While voices grow and die,
for rights and justice,
for fake promises,
for another false paradise.
We will suck, and soak and burn each
other,
Until the end of this nightmare.

-----167-----

Role of people pleasure ends,
Let's unfollow all trends,
If you know what makes you laugh,
Doing that won't be so tough.

Take charge of your story now,
Glory wakes who cares how,
It's your chance to flow and shine,

Self-believer you old wine.

Late bloomer you'll stay here long,
Singing everlasting song,
Morning's Manifestation light,
Knows your heart's purpose bright.

-----168-----

Another way around the maze,
Changed my thoughts new gaze,
Life I wanna create,
Heal me through my fate.
Drifted away from dream,
Heart knows silent scream,
Destiny grew inside,
Heal my ego my pride.
Love loves moonlit bloom,
Soul crossed dark night's gloom,
Purpose appeared near,
Heal my doubts my fear.

-----169-----
Time knows when right time,
Past shifts new paradigm,
Through your heart so divine,

Show me love feminine.
You were there always,
Guided path new ways,
No matter mind in doubt,
Silenced deep dark shout.
Now my head is blank,
Destiny upgrades rank,
Hold me till I flow,
In your eyes I glow.

-----170-----

Toxic dream dark waves,
Long lost love still craves,
Blue smoke desires shine,
Good bye fear of mine.
Destiny shows at last,
Now I feel my trust,
Time to build from core,
Learned to manifest more.
Castle of secret found,
Key words make known sound,
Soon I'll crack the code,
Walk on self-made road.

-----171-----

Take my colors and shine,
Full moon glows as your third eye,
New you on destined path.

-----172-----

This dark brown peace stays,
Silence grows dream ways,
Love you cast goes deep,
One more light year's sleep !!!
Music smiles once more,
Cords melt dry heart's core,
Tones of joy smells raw,
On your soul I draw.

-----173-----

Mistry mountain's call,
Déjà vu moments stall.
Here before I was.
Back again with my cause.
Chaotic games time play.
Till you learn and slay,
Doubts and fears within,
Advance gratitude's win.

Path knows souls' purpose,
Clouds shine on dark grass,
Blue rock dream guides through,
Will remain all along true.

-----174-----

Magical lights of sound,
Purple love unbound,
Dreamy shades stay for a while,
Sing along morning smile.

Goddesses spread their wings,
Keep quiet gloomy dark things,
Time kissed chords unnamed,
My Sun soul untamed.

Knowledge is dry old past,
Not known wide and vast,
Many more births to die,
Sing along love that's why.

-----175-----

Let her rest a little,
While dream writes a to do list,
Waking up is so easy.

-----176-----
Path once loved and lost,
Eyes still search mind frost,
Destiny changes course,
Dark dreams awakened force.
Path will show right way,
Find clues awake you stay,
Look closely to see,
Deep root thoughts mind tree.
Known face unknown joy,
Time breaks desire toy,
Forgotten rain pours dream,
Love flows through hate stream.

-----177-----
Moonshine on clouds clears doubts,
Dawn will take care of all memories,
Love will find sky again.

-----178-----
Wet mind on dry dream,
Graffiti clouds now scream,
Lazy noon draws soft stroke,
Eve waits till morn broke.
Silly love songs sounds sweet,
Autumn's breezy green treat!

-----179-----
Dream within a dream,
Endless soft torn scream,
You came now you're gone,
Shadow cloud melts to morn.

Come light let's play a game,
New tale for old name,
No matter who says what,
Don't stop once you start.

They thought they know you,
Truth smiled soaked in dew,
Take time world moves slow,
Go deep let dream glow.

-----180-----
Let go you from "You",
No matter what says who,
How can lost be found?
Truth was safe and sound.
Pause and feel the soul,
Many worlds but one goal.
Stick around let joy guide,
stand by your own side.
Look for clues unknown,
Mind speaks guidance shown,
Follow dreams unlock mode,
That's you and your code.

-----181-----
Transformation sign,
Now need what is mine,
Golden morning shows,
My path destiny knows.
You showed what once lost,
Time has paid that cost,
Love will help to grow,
Joy boat now we row.
Luck awaited to be found,
Mind stopped and turned around,
With monsoons first rain,
Let's wash all past's stain.

-----182-----
Your warmth in my heart
Followed one dream from the ocean's
deep
So far yet so close.

-----183-----
And then came the guardian
To take you out
Of your comfort zone.
"It's time " he said.
Your awaken third eye gazed
softly to the shadow of this
Warrior of light.
Known from another time,
Another birth.

-----184-----
Change my name at last,
Your seed to my roots many worlds,
Come to me new wind.

-----185-----
Shadow loves to misguide mind,
Body knows how to trust in nature,
Universe connects with soul.

-----186-----
The color of your grace,
Creates new leaves in the morning
spring,
Every day is yours now.

-----187-----
Wear that face to lie,
Silence will show more than you know,
Look within for the truth.

-----188-----
Lines of thoughts and dreams,
You float while ego screams,
My muse tell me more,
Mind's tale kept in store.
Ink blue sometimes black,
Light will pass through crack,
Till then we shall dance,

Life drops moment's chance.
Shots of you brings joy,
Lost lane forgotten toy,
Love sings morning breeze,
Fly high leave known trees.

-----189-----
Sunday afternoon grey crow shadows,
Looking through the surprised eyes born new,
Days will bring innocent joy.

-----190-----
Morning wipes night's moist eyes,
Then you know something gotta change soon,
Darkness is just a tone.

Cover page Illustration Nilanjan Das

Muse - Mariana Marín Arenas